The Pivo Tour of Slovakia

Memoirs of an Anglo-Slovak Student Exchange
The Observations of an Outsider

MIKE FOX

Copyright © 2019 by Mike Fox
All rights reserved. No part of this book may be reproduced, scanned, or distributed in any printed or electronic form without permission.
First Edition: August 2019
Printed in the United States of America
ISBN: 1645504611
ISBN: 9781645504610

Contents

Prologue
Why did I ever go on this trip? vii

Saturday 1 April
Getting the Show on the Road 1

Sunday 2 April
Calais to Nürnberg 3

Monday 3 April
We finally make it to Slovakia 6

Tuesday 4 April
First impressions of the college and the town of Trenčín 9

Wednesday 5 April
Excursion to Bratislava, Slovakia's capital city 13

Thursday 6 April
A Castle, a Football Match and Children's Town 18

Friday 7 April
Journeying up the Vah Valley 23

Saturday 8 April
Walking in the High Tatras 29

Sunday 9 April
The Low Tatras and the 'Fossilised' Village of Cicimani 34

Monday 10 April
Questions at the Town Hall and a Fashion Show 38

Tuesday 11 April
    A Spot of Bother in Nürnberg 45

Wednesday 12 April
    Crossing Western Europe 47

Thursday 13 April
    Return to Albion 48

Postscript
    Comments made by Students and Staff on the Pivo Tour ... 49

Prologue

WHY DID I EVER GO ON THIS TRIP?

I am not a lecturer at South Devon College, and I never have been. I certainly wasn't a student in 1995, the year of the Pivo Trip, at least not in the conventional sense. So why was I the one person who was invited on the trip but didn't really fit into a recognised role? (The trip, by the way, was a student exchange between SPSS College, Trenčín, Slovakia and South Devon College, Torbay, England.)

It all started a few years earlier, when one of the lecturers from South Devon College, an architect by the name of Chris, rang me at my office in the local Council (where I was working at the time), and asked if he could bring some French students to the Town Hall to learn about the British planning system and how we 'did' it locally. Apparently, he initially asked one of my colleagues to do it; the colleague, however, declined to get involved, but he gave Chris my name, as someone "*who likes that sort of thing*". The group of French students duly came over to see how we 'did' planning over here, and I stepped into a new relationship.

I gave the lecture as requested, in appalling French it has to be said, to what turned out to be a very gracious group of students from Brittany. Shortly after my lecture, I rashly volunteered the information that I was quite interested in the French planning system. This in turn led to an invitation for me to accompany a set of students from South

Devon College for the return trip to visit their counterparts in St Brieuc in Brittany a couple of weeks later.

One thing led to another, and I found myself being invited to another trip to Brittany a year later, followed by two field trips to Paris in subsequent years. Then Martin, one of the college lecturers and the leader of the group, said that in the following year, he was planning to take a group of students from the college to Slovakia; was I interested in coming along? It took me a few nano-seconds to decide that I was very keen to be a member of this group, especially as I had never been to Eastern Europe. It turned out to be a memorable experience for (mostly) the right reasons.

Pivo, by the way, is the Slovak word for beer, and the whole adventure became known as the Pivo Trip for rather obvious reasons.

Saturday 1 April

GETTING THE SHOW ON THE ROAD

It is 5:30 in the evening and Torquay is bathing in bright sunshine. We have been led to believe that the temperatures in Slovakia at this time of the year could be as low as minus 6 degrees Celsius, and the early evening sunshine in South Devon is appreciated.

Our coach sets off from South Devon College at six o'clock amidst a bevy of waving parents and friends. Some of the students break the ice by challenging the lecturers to a game of trivial pursuit; a few of the other students appear to be the worse for wear after imbibing unknown but in some cases, significant quantities of alcohol, and they are asleep by the time we reach the next-door town of Newton Abbot, about 20 minutes into our long journey. Back to the trivial pursuit, Martin, the leader of the exchange trip, succeeds in winning before we hit the M25 motorway, around Greater London.

The ferry port of Dover is reached by one o'clock in the morning; Dover Castle looks impressive as it is lit up in the dark sky. Tony, one of the lecturers who is an architect, says he is not convinced that the castle is as attractive or interesting enough to visit during daylight, but in the small hours it looks pretty impressive to me.

Our Channel crossing is calm, although I think I detect a marked drop in the temperature somewhere in mid-channel, but maybe this is the climatic effect of the water. The ferry draws into Calais harbour at 03:15 hours local French time. As many of us chatted for the duration of the crossing, I have had no sleep at this point since leaving Torquay; and a new day is dawning.

Sunday 2 April

CALAIS TO NÜRNBERG

At daybreak, our coach pulls into a service station just within Germany. Sarah, the only female lecturer on the trip, has been sensible enough to sleep. As she awakens, she wants to know if we are in the Netherlands, which we all find amusing, though it's not that funny really. At our first stop at a service station, the German coffee tastes good, especially so early in the morning.

Several hours later, and the German autobahns are getting busy; Germany appears to be more 'switched on' on a Sunday than Britain. We cross the River Rhine on a high bridge. Frankfurt airport is busy; at least four planes can be spotted flying low overhead as we drive alongside the Lufthansa Terminal building.

The scenery becomes more undulating and wooded as we press on eastwards towards Nürnberg. At another autobahn service stop, out comes the students' football. One of the students cracks a joke about watching out for unexploded World War Two bombs; don't they realise most Germans can understand English?

Back on the coach, several videos, mainly featuring the Blues Brothers, are put on to make the journey pass more quickly. Many of us, me included, doze off for a couple of hours as the coach drives along busy autobahns.

We approach the city of Nürnberg by mid-afternoon, but the location of the youth hostel is not immediately obvious to our driver. A small sketch map (from where I'm not sure) comes to the rescue and we circumnavigate the ancient city wall, eventually spotting the medieval castle. We book into the youth hostel, which is situated inside the castle, at 3:00pm.

The Alt Stadt (old town) of Nürnberg spreads out beneath the castle. In the central square, large photographs the size of advertisement hoardings, show the extent of the devastation caused by the World War Two bombing of the city. They also illustrate just how impressive has been the reconstruction of this beautiful historic area in the post-war years, now looking every inch the undisturbed medieval centre of this large city.

Everyone in our group is impressed with the youth hostel where we will be staying the night. In particular the high-pressure showers are appreciated. Our cold evening meal is substantial and enjoyable.

We absorb the 'Alt Stadt' in our evening walk. The overall sense of harmony in the townscape is striking. There are lots of variations on a theme without excessive regimentation, including attractive roof cadences. The city centre has extensive areas of pedestrianisation, together with separately identified cycleways. Some of our students haven't got to grips with the cycleway markings and find themselves caught out unawares by remonstrating cyclists.

Hauptmarket Square, with its Schöner Brunnen statue, seems to be the focal point of the city. A lively market is in full swing, with lots of noise and colour. We amble over the River Peguitz on the Fleischbrücke Bridge, where we can see haunting views of arches, bridges and attractive waterfront buildings. Lorenzkirche Platz is another beautiful square.

The city does have its 'ordinary' areas as well. Walking down the Köningstrasse towards the station, we pass some rather bland 'anywhere' signs and shopfronts, but perhaps we are being hypercritical.

Nürnberg main railway station is not only a superb monument to the celebration of rail travel, but it is an impressive hub to a complex public transport system that most British towns and cities would die for (well, almost). It is obvious from observing on the ground and from pouring over maps back in the youth hostel that Nürnberg has a well-integrated transport system, with u-bahns (underground trains), s-bahns (trams), railways, buses, cycle ways and well-connected pedestrian routes.

We return from the station back through the historic core and come across yet another impressive square – Lorenzer Platz – which contains an interesting juxtaposition of the old and the new. We re-cross the river at Museumbrücke and end up in a friendly pub, which has an even friendlier German customer, who insists on buying drinks for everyone in our party. Three of us get the short straw and make polite conversation with him.

In addition to its impressive communications system on terra firma, Nürnberg also has a port on the Europa Canal, a vital waterway which links up with the Rhine and the Danube. The large youth hostel map of the city also shows rail links between the port and the national rail network. It is all very 'joined up', to use an overused phrase in vogue at the moment.

The city of Nürnberg is surrounded by woodland to the north, east and south. Its ancient city walls are intact in places and impressively so. As far as I can tell, the 'middle wall' is almost completely intact, complete with moat, defensive towers and castle.

Martin, Tony and I are sharing a bedroom in the roof of the castle, and we are in our bunks by 9:30pm. Some of the students return from a night on the tiles in good voice at around 00:45 hrs. I count five of them from our upper storey vantage point, but they subsequently maintain there were only four of them.

Monday 3 April

WE FINALLY MAKE IT TO SLOVAKIA

We are breakfasted and out of the youth hostel by 08:30 hrs. Our coach crawls through the Nüremberg morning rush hour before picking up the autobahn to Ravensberg and then on to Passau at the Austrian border.

The Bavarian countryside is pleasantly undulating; rolling hills punctuated by tightly clustered villages, each focusing on a church which invariably features a clock tower. Some of these churches have onion-shaped domes and are beautifully coloured. They seem to create a visual sermon of praise for the Creator of the Good Earth.

We cross over the border into Austria and bypass the industrial city of Linz. Our highway is running through a wide valley with a flat floor, and there are occasional hints of mountains in the distance. (This is definitely not picture-postcard Austria.) At a service station we come across a Muslim toilet and wash room. Martin asks why the Austrians should single out separate treatment for Muslims, but it may be that the Islamic community itself requested separate loos. But they serve as a reminder of how far east we have travelled.

The landscape becomes more varied and interesting as we approach Vienna. Even as close as 15 kilometres away from the city centre, we are still driving through rural, undulating and largely wooded scenery. Then the motorway takes a turn round a pronounced bend – and the huge city of Vienna is spread out before us, much of it gleaming white in the sun, with a few futuristic high-rise towers silhouetted in the distance. Before long, we are skirting this great city on the Vienna ring road, reaching to within five kilometres of the city centre as we drive along an elevated section of the highway. Not much Baroque architecture can be seen from where we are travelling. A sense of frustration develops – at least by me – we are so near and yet so far from seeing the beautiful parts of this historic city.

A choice has to be made as our coach approaches the Slovakian border. Martin opts to fork right, which turns out to be the scenic as opposed to the direct route. It is also signed as the road to Budapest! Martin is now associated with Budapest for the remainder of the trip.

The border of the Slovak Republic comes into view. It's a 'hard' crossing, the first of any formality, as we come to the edge of the European Union. One of our students, Peggy from Taiwan, has to step down from our coach and progress through immigration control, and Sarah, one of our leaders, accompanies her. The rest of us remain on the coach, contemplating Peggy's fate. It seems a long wait, but in fact we are through the border controls, with Peggy back inside the coach, in under half an hour.

We cross the not-so-blue River Danube and immediately enter Bratislava, Slovakia's capital city. Now there is a noticeable drop in the volume of traffic on the roads, and the numbers of vehicles plummet even further after we leave the capital behind and progress northwards. Our motorway follows the Vah River valley all the way to Trenčín. This town will be our main base in Slovakia. Our highway runs parallel to a well-used electrified railway, especially by long freight trains.

The site of a new nuclear power station comes into view on the left, apparently designed by the creators of Chernobyl, and shortly to be commissioned. Our coach enters the town of Trenčín and parks at the SPSS College, whose students we will be interacting with over our stay in Slovakia. It is five o'clock in the evening as we step out of the coach.

The students are farmed out to their host families, and afterwards we have our first meal at the college hostel. The leaders' bedrooms, including mine, are situated on the sixth floor of this huge, utilitarian, concrete structure. Although Tony and I have separate bedrooms, we have shared shower and toilet facilities, which is not unusual in a student context, I guess. In fact, we are informed that during term time, four students would sleep in my room, and two in Tony's room. A welcome bottle of mineral water sits on the table. I have a balcony, which looks out over the town, taking in the distinctive castle.

After dinner, the leaders and coach drivers are invited round to a bar owned by a lady called Beata, who is the senior organiser on the Slovak side of the exchange, and she is also our interpreter. The bar is located in her back garden. Tony asks me if it would have been granted planning permission in England! (I think most English local planning authorities might have something to say about impact on neighbouring living conditions…)

In the bar we spend a lot of time discussing our trip and plans for the next ten days. I am given a glass of a spirit by the name of 'borravitchka' – and quickly decide that a couple of sips is preferable to swallowing the lot. I then make do with a couple of 'pivos' (beers). It's a good, convivial evening which stretches well into the night and then into the small hours, with a lot of conversation as we all get to know each other. Somehow, we manage to find our way back to our hostel through dark streets and past a lot of barking dogs. I am in bed by 02:30 hrs.

Tuesday 4 April

FIRST IMPRESSIONS OF THE COLLEGE AND THE TOWN OF TRENČÍN

My alarm shatters my dreams at 06:45 hrs, and it is an early breakfast at just gone seven. Afterwards we are taken for a tour round the college. I drop a bottle of mineral water in one of the corridors, but the Slovak students assure me it is not a problem and cheerfully clean up the mess. I really must be more careful.

Both sets of students carry out a joint surveying exercise in the lecture theatre. It involves calculating and drawing the course of values of transverse strengths and moments of bend on a set construction (which I glean from reading the instructions). The Slovak students are very keen to assist our group, and on the face of it, appear more knowledgeable in this field of knowledge (certainly more knowledgeable than me, which perhaps is not saying a great deal).

The leaders (including me) are ushered out of the lecture theatre and into a reception in the office of the college principal, Mr Strubner. Food and drinks are set out for us. We are all feeling under the weather (probably coach lag). Our leader, Martin, seems especially jaded and even refuses the offer of more beer. (He is even heard saying that he is giving up beer for good, although absolutely no one in the room believes him.)

Some of our students already have quasi-horror stories to tell about their accommodation. Shane, for example, tells us that he had to make three bus journeys, followed by a two-mile walk to get to his adoptive home for out here. Last night, he says, it was so dark alighting from one of the buses that he couldn't see his hand. This morning, he left his accommodation at half past six and arrived at the college at eight. "This has got to be a wind up!" he says.

At 11:30 in the morning we regroup with the students back in the lecture theatre and watch two films (in Slovak); one covers the implementation of a housing estate, and the other focuses on the development of a roof garden. Some of the English students are showing advanced signs of boredom. One of them has just thrown up outside the lecture theatre (linked I think to the activities of last night rather than the impact of the films).

The roof garden video has now been running for 30 minutes, and we are have not progressed beyond laying the bitumen. Several of our students are now discussing a football match which has been arranged for this coming Thursday between the English and Slovak students. Outside, the sun is shining; apparently, yesterday, our day of arrival, was the first warm day of the year in Trenčín, and we haven't seen any snow in Slovakia. In fact, the weather has been glorious ever since we left Torquay.

In the afternoon I take my first walk into the town centre, which takes around 20 minutes. En route, I ask someone in the street in my best Slovak if they speak English, as I still haven't found the centre. The guy replies in perfect English and accompanies me into the town centre. He says he is the editor of the local newspaper in Trenčín and he shows great interest in our visit. I inform him that we are due to meet Trenčín's chief executive later in the afternoon, and he says that he will be there.

I also strike up a conversation with a young woman in a bookshop. She speaks good English with an American accent, and she also tells me that she is accompanying us on our trip to Bratislava tomorrow. Her name is Helena, and she is to be one of our interpreters for most of our time in Slovakia.

At four o'clock, a small group of us travel from the college to the town hall, which is a contemporary looking concrete building in the town centre. We are welcomed by the chief executive of the local council and served with coffee. I am already developing quite a taste for Slovak coffee, which is strong and delicious. The chief executive then provides us with a long list of key facts about the municipality of Trenčín, including announcing a plan to enable commercial traffic to come up the river Vah from the Danube as far as Trenčín.

You get the idea that the guy is quite proud of his town. Interestingly, the thing he omits to say is that Trenčín is a major military base, which is possibly its biggest economic asset. Our meeting is attended by local reporters and journalists. My editor friend from earlier in the day is in attendance.

A question and answer session gets underway. A wide range of issues are discussed, including the twinning proposals with other boroughs; promoting Trenčín abroad; tourism as a catalyst for development; a five-year plan for growth in Trenčín, which is being undertaken in collaboration with a Dutch university; Trenčín's unitary status as a borough; and finally, local authority financial problems. I detect a slight air of disbelief when we say that local government is experiencing severe financial problems in Britain and it's not just a problem in Slovakia. I wonder whether they all think the streets are paved in gold in the UK.

We discuss the issue of tourism, particularly in relation to conservation, and the danger of indiscriminate development which could threaten to destroy the very qualities that the tourists come to see in Trenčín.

I join Martin, Tony, Sarah and Beata for a stroll in the historic core of Trenčín. Beata points out the memorial to the Great Plague that nearly wiped out Trenčín in the Middle Ages; except that she pronounces it is the great 'plaque', and I have visions of medieval dental problems. We see examples of both sympathetic and not-so-sympathetic infill development facing the main square, which goes by the name of Mierove Namastie. We walk back to our hostel, crossing the River Vah on a steel-girdered bridge, which also carries a railway.

Over dinner, Martin explains that the college hostel was completed in August 1968, just as the Czechoslovakian uprising was being brutally crushed by the Soviet army. Apparently, the Soviets intended to use the new building as a barracks, but within 24 hours of this intention being made known to the wider populace, students from all over Czechoslovakia came and occupied the building in passive resistance. As a result, Soviet soldiers never slept in the building. So tonight, I am sleeping in a bit of Cold War history.

In the evening we are taken out for drinks by two of the Slovak lecturers, Doncan and Jan. We end up in a bar situated down in a basement near the Hotel Tatra in the centre of Trenčín. Later we are joined by several of our students and their new Slovak friends. By now, it is clear that Martin has forgotten his commitment to an alcohol-free existence for the rest of eternity. The Pivo Trip is back on track, as it were. I decide to lay off the 'fire water' tonight – just black coffee and beer.

Wednesday 5 April

EXCURSION TO BRATISLAVA, SLOVAKIA'S CAPITAL CITY

I awake to the sounds of Eric Clapton's *Don't you know my name?* which is coming out over the tannoi system. Martin comes into my room just before breakfast in a better frame of mind than yesterday (Then I am not sure he would have known his name at 07:00 hrs!)

After another pork breakfast everyone in the group boards our coach to Bratislava, the capital city of Slovakia, population circa 400,000. Until the start of the Second World War, the city had a sizeable population of both Germans and Jews.

Helena, the young lady I met yesterday in the bookshop, joins Beata as our second interpreter, and we set off for Bratislava. We experience considerable difficulty trying to find a coach parking space in the downtown area, and our driver is distinctly unimpressed when one of our students, Jason, asks why we are driving around in circles. Finally, we find a large enough space opposite the offices of Slovak Radio, which occupies a building resembling an inverted pyramid.

We alight from the coach and divide into two groups. Tony takes a group with him to visit the architecture faculty of the University of Bratislava. The rest of us, following Helena, enter the oldest part of the city along the Obchodna, which is a dedicated area for pedestrians, but with tram tracks slicing through, so you can't switch off from traffic and relax completely.

Bratislava's historic core starts to the south of a main street by the name of Slovensko, where we descend down into narrow, cobbled streets, passing under arches and negotiating sharp bends. The street eventually opens out into small squares, which are dominated by Hungarian Baroque architecture. We turn into another medieval street, Michalski, which crosses a bridge over the remains of the city moat; then we make our way back through the city gate, to where we started our walking tour of Old Bratislava.

I take Sarah and Helena for a cup of coffee, which costs me in the region of 40p, in what appears to be an up-market café with pleasant surroundings. Afterwards, we learn that most of the students went for a pizza, a couple of blocks away from us.

After our short break we descend into a beautiful pedestrianised square, Hiavne Namastie, which is overlooked by an elegant church tower. Passing through an arch, we enter Primaciane Square, in time to see the changing of the guard, with the replacement set of soldiers goose-stepping into position.

In the midst of all these photo-opportunities, my camera starts to play up. Helena helpfully finds a pharmacist's shop and she explains the problem with my camera. They can't do anything, and I buy another film. In the meantime, we have lost the rest of our group; Helena says she feels responsible and guilty, when in fact she is being helpful. Initially, she doesn't seem too sure about exactly where our coach is, but we eventually spot the inverted pyramid of the Radio Slovak HQ and we can relax. We pass by some beggars whom we saw earlier, before we retraced our steps, sitting and squatting in exactly the same positions as when we first saw them several hours earlier.

After eating a late lunch by the coach, we visit Bratislava Castle, situated on a hill where it enjoys panoramic views over the Danube and across into the Austrian countryside. Below us, a single span cantilever bridge, built in 1974, impressively spans the river. Known as the SNP Bridge, *Bridge of the Slovak National Uprising*, it has opened up the south side of the Danube for the development of an urban extension to Bratislava. This large, monolithic development by the name of Petrazalka is now home to

150,000 inhabitants. The primary schools in this huge development, so we are told, don't have names but numbers. Why? I wonder.

The Austrian hills are clearly visible to the south-west, and a huge oil refinery/petro-chemical complex can be seen in the distance to the south-east. A steady stream of commercial traffic plies up and down the river. A large barge passes by, heading in the direction of Vienna, displaying the Romanian flag.

The Slovak National Assembly sits next to the castle. Although it is a striking modern building, its setting is almost suburban, reminiscent of a new civic centre in one of the outer London Boroughs. The Assembly sits opposite a leafy green and a row of terraced houses. The whole vista seems very quaint for a building of such national importance.

Our Slovak guide informs us that the approach road to the new SNP Danube Bridge obliterated an old Jewish quarter of the city. Apparently, there were some 95,000 Jews living in what is now Slovakia before World War Two; now, at the time of our visit, there are less than 3,000. There seems to be reluctance on the part of our guide to talk about the Jews in Slovakia and what happened to them during the war. Our questions to the guide about this get us nowhere.

In Bratislava, we are informed that more historic buildings have been demolished after the Second World War than during it. But attitudes towards conservation of older buildings are now changing in a positive direction.

Bratislava Castle has four towers, their configuration giving it the look of an upside-down dining table. In a land full of outstanding castles, this one, I am afraid to say, does not make it into the premier league, although it occupies an important vantage point with a commanding view up and down the Danube which was no doubt an important strategic advantage in bygone times.

Looking down from the castle, the Blue Danube Hotel on the riverside, adjacent to the Danube Bridge, has the look of a successful development, although the demolition of the Jewish Quarter to make way for it seems to me to be an unacceptable price to have to pay for this development.

Our coach takes us to a parking space down by the banks of the Danube, adjacent to the Slovakian National Museum. A small group of us then meander through several narrow streets to Hriezdoslavovo Square, which is spacious, graceful and tree lined. Helena interprets for us in several shops. I buy a Slovak T shirt for £12.

We bump into several more of our students, who enthusiastically tell us that they have caused a bar to run out of beer. Perhaps a more likely interpretation of events is that the bar is refusing to serve any more beer to English students.

What are my first impressions of this newly designated capital city, following the break-up of the former Czechoslovakia? The fine urban grain of much of Bratislava's historic core is thankfully intact, with the notable exception of what was the Jewish Quarter. Some of the inner areas just outside the oldest parts of the city appear to have a French influence, possibly dating from the nineteenth century. The extent of pedestrian priority areas and streets with limited vehicular access is also impressive. However, not all of the infill development is in sensitive harmony with the older buildings, and some of the historic structures are looking very neglected. Loose cobblestones are a hazard. A few enhancement schemes in these areas would not come amiss.

The city has experienced several ethnic shifts in relatively recent history. It was part of the Austro-Hungarian Empire until the end of the First World War, when Hungarians formed the majority population. During the inter-war years, 80 % of the city's inhabitants were German. Since World War Two there has been a Soviet influence – at least until very recently. The present Slovak majority is quite a recent thing, and the city seems to have an identity crisis; whose identity is being preserved?

On our return journey to Trenčín, we stop at a small settlement called Piestany, which is a spa town on the River Vah. We walk around an island in the river where the spa is situated. Silent bicycles whizzing past you at something significantly greater than running speed are the biggest health hazard here. Piestany's pleasant verdant setting is reputedly good for recuperation. Apparently, the river mud is smeared over patients who have skin problems. Quite a number of the clients appear to be from the Middle East. Some of the gardens and trees in this place look very English, and the small town has a peaceful atmosphere; an oasis of calm.

Our coach carries on up the opposite (eastern) side of the valley from the main Bratislava road, travelling close to the foothills which define the valley side. This is altogether the less busy and more tranquil side of the valley. At one point, a spectacular castle can be seen, perched on a limestone crag and it appears that restoration works are being carried out on it.

Shortly afterwards, Jason, one of our students, asks out loud what the Slovak word 'dovidenia' means. It means 'goodbye' in English. Sarah then comments, loudly enough for everyone in the coach to hear, that this is the word all the Slovak girls have been telling him, which amuses us for the rest of the journey to Trenčín.

None of the leaders go out drinking tonight. Sarah, Tony and I go for a stroll through Trenčín, and we discover a downtown restaurant near to the Hotel Tatra. We somehow succeed in breaking the language barrier and manage to order salad, steak and chips, plus beer, coke and coffees, all for the price of £1 each.

In the meantime, the students have been organising a disco and we are probably the first to get to bed.

Thursday 6 April

A CASTLE, A FOOTBALL MATCH AND CHILDREN'S TOWN

In the morning we pay a visit to Trenčín Castle, where the English and Slovak students are taking part in a joint surveying exercise. The castle is a prominent landmark as you approach the town, and it protrudes improbably and spectacularly from the side of a limestone escarpment. Unsurprisingly then, the castle commands fine views of the town and provides longer vistas up and down the Vah Valley. It is a visual reminder that Trenčín has had a military significance since the Romans won a decisive battle here in AD 179 under the Emperor Marcus Aurelius.

The present castle artefacts date from the fourteenth century and the site has been fought over and besieged several times during its long history. The Soviet Hammer and Sickle flag flew from the top of the castle tower until recent times, when a famous wall in a more famous city came down, heralding the end of the Cold War.

In the fourteenth century, the waters of the River Vah lapped against the castle walls. In the intervening years, the course of the river has shifted 200 metres to the west, and the historic core of the town of Trenčín sits between the castle walls and the river.

The layout of the castle includes both an inner and outer bailey. The main building in the castle complex comprises a series of rooms of widely varying dimensions, which are connected by steep (and in some cases, very steep) steps and staircases. To refer to the internal arrangement of the castle as 'labyrinthine' would not be an exaggeration. The castle tower reaches up to a height of around 20-25 metres above the natural summit of the crag.

This location, looking down from the castle, is by far the best place to take in views of the town, which now spreads along the river. From this vantage point, Ivan and one of his lecturer colleagues explain, with the help of one of the interpreters, some of the principal features of Trenčín. The river and its floodplain have been instrumental in influencing Trenčín's urban form, although in recent years a 'new town' has been developed well away from the river, to the east of the castle.

The River Vah sweeps majestically through the town. It is a major barrier to movement, as the river is crossed by only one road and one railway bridge. At present, only pleasure craft use the river, and a small marina can be seen on one of the islands. There is talk however of possible dredging and improvement of the river's navigation to enable commercial traffic to come upstream to Trenčín from the Danube.

Trenčín is a railway junction on the main line from Bratislava to the northern industrial towns in Slovakia, and a lot of freight goes by rail over here. The local economy centres on the army (there is a prominent barracks in the town), electric power generation (housed in buildings resembling the architecture of civic buildings or law courts), and the town has a range of industries including textiles, machine tools and an export clothing business. There are several large schools and colleges. Trenčín is also the main shopping centre serving a wide hinterland. All in all, you get the impression of an industrious and confident town on the move.

I think the town has a mosque, although the interpreter describes it as: "a synagogue for the Turks". There is an old synagogue in the town, which has been converted into a school.

On the western side of the floodplain, the motorway which we travelled along on our first day is being extended further up the valley. The motorway will bypass Trenčín, which clearly could impact on some forms of trade. The new highway is expected to be up and running next year at a cost of 200 million crowns (£4 million) for around 3 miles of road. This compares favourably with the UK where, for example, Stage

3 of the Torbay Ring Road is costing £15 million over a distance of 1.5 miles (if it ever gets constructed).

Immediately to the south-east of the castle there is a forest, which acts as a foil to the castle itself. It also performs the role of a green wedge between the old and new towns of Trenčín. Hopefully, this important area will remain free from new development.

Trenčín also boasts an impressive ice rink; the local team has just lost the national championship ice hockey title and they were runners-up last year as well. The town also has a football stadium, swimming pool and an indoor sports hall.

Back at the castle, Ivan invites me to partake of a cup of black Slovakian coffee, and he explains the restoration work on the castle, some of which he has been carrying out with the aid of lots of photographs. The work still hasn't been completed, although attempts at refurbishment started as long ago as the 1930s, and the current programme started in 1956. It is clearly a vocation for Ivan, and he even met the woman who became his wife at the castle, although the story goes that the first time he met her, they had an argument over whether and how much she should pay to enter the castle! Clearly relationships have thawed since then.

Lack of regular funding means the restoration work on the castle is intermittent. Some revenue comes from visiting tourists. There are official tour guides and a limited amount of tourism development has taken place. Objects such as swords, plaques and scrolls ranging from battles to pillage through to ceremonial scenes and court life reside in glass cases in various rooms in the tower.

We leave the tower and I take several photographs of the students working on various projects throughout the castle grounds. They all look industrious, at least from a distance. Sarah tells us about the myth of Princess Fatima; it is connected to the well in the castle courtyard, and it does not have a happy ending.

The afternoon is taken up with the Anglo-Slovak football competition, which the students have been talking about since we got here. This generates much excitement among the local population, and a lot of spectators appear on the balconies of the girls' hostel which overlooks the pitch. Team photographs are taken as the teams line up on the pitch, Wembley style. Then the two national anthems are sung; no attention to detail is spared.

Two English teams play each other first, and Martin's team wins. His team includes Tony and Sarah. Sarah allegedly fouls one of the students, Jason, who hasn't stopped talking about it since. Our two teams eventually finish second and third in the overall competition. In the final, the Slovak team wins, despite the local referee supporting the away team at every opportunity.

Immediately after the football tournament, one of our students, Leigh, jumps into a swimming pool, dislocates a shoulder and is taken to hospital. "*I was doing the crawl and it just popped out!*" is Leigh's explanation.

In the evening, Martin invites Tony, Sarah and me to visit a nearby orphanage called Children's Town. We are introduced to one of the orphanage's house parents, Kvetto, who also manages the entire place, and his 18-year-old daughter, Lucy, on the steps of the college hostel. Lucy speaks excellent English, and she tells us that she is studying English and Philosophy at Nitra University in the south of Slovakia. Kvetto is a well built, bearded man with a quiet authority about him.

Kvetto drives us up to Children's Town, which lies on the outskirts of Trenčín. It is home to children aged 3-18 years, and it has one child/young person in each age cohort; their parents have either died or are unable to cope with looking after their son or daughter. We are shown around the children's village complex by Kvetto's deputy. There are 17 families living on the campus, in addition to a school which takes in pupils from the surrounding community as well as from Children's Town.

As we walk through the complex, we come across a group of children singing folk songs; not all of them are girls, and one of them has the appearance of a gypsy. We also see children doing weight training and taking part in a very competitive game of volleyball (a sport in which Slovaks excel). The atmosphere is relaxed, and the children are clearly enjoying their activities. They seem to have overcome the institutional atmosphere, and this has been replaced with a 'family feel', which is impressive to observe, even if it is difficult to precisely define.

After our mini-tour, our host family invites us back to their home. We notice that all the foster children's bedrooms are immaculately tidy, but without any obvious sign of regimentation, at least to my untrained eyes. Some of the children are watching television as we make our introductions. One or two try out their English on us.

We are introduced to Kvetto's wife, and to the family dog, which appears to be overwhelmed by all the extra people. We are invited to sit around a glass table, which accommodates an array of drinks and savouries. Kvetto and his family are very welcoming and hospitable – perhaps too hospitable, when it comes to liquid refreshment! Having been so impressed by their caring work and friendliness, I have no option but to down a glass of 50% proof borrovicka, which hits my stomach with the force of an Exocet missile. And in hindsight, I am not sure going onto a superb red wine shortly afterwards is such a good idea. The traditional Slovak hospitality which we are receiving (a bit like the way the Chinese do it) means that my glass is continuously refilled.

The conversation around the table is lively and animated. We talk about the mutual perceptions of our two countries, the Slovak language, Shakespeare, dogs, politics, Catholic and Protestant theology, our jobs and, of course, seeing where we are, some of the challenges and problems of fostering children. Kvetto can speak good English, and Lucy is fluent – after only four years of learning, so she tells me. Somehow, Martin manages to squeeze in some of his jokes, and Kvetto retaliates with some Slovak jokes – for Irishman, read Czech…..

It is a thoroughly enjoyable evening. We are all in good spirits, seemingly without a care in the world. My ego swells when Lucy (entirely unsolicited) tells me that I pronounce Slovak well (based on the half a dozen words or so that I know, so I really shouldn't get too carried away on this score).

Time passes quickly. All good things, however, come to an end, and at around 10pm, Martin reminds us that he has promised to call in at Beata's bar (the Regatta). We say goodbye to Children's Town, drive back to the college hostel, and then we walk to Beata's bar where we are offered yet more drinks. I down another couple of black coffees. We walk back to our sleeping quarters, past all the barking dogs and we are ensconced in our rooms by midnight. It's been quite a day and we all seem quite animated.

The weather has changed during the day. It was quite cold this morning while we were at the castle, and then it changed into a sunny afternoon. Then, in the early evening, while we walked around Children's Town, we experienced a ten-minute shower. The word is that snow is falling on the Tatras Mountains, and I fall asleep thinking that perhaps we are in for a shock in the morning.

Friday 7 April

JOURNEYING UP THE VAH VALLEY

This day is going to have a number of twists and turns. As we leave for the Tatras Mountains, we have Jan as our guide. It was going to be Kvetto, but he was taken ill overnight. Beata cannot be with us, as she has family commitments, so Kvetto's daughter, Lucy, is drafted in, and at the last minute, word is sent to Helena, giving her just ten minutes to pack her bags and join us as our second interpreter.

Jan sits immediately behind me in the coach and points out features along the route with great frequency, using Lucy as interpreter. He certainly is a mine of information. Helena perches down on the 'gangway' step next to the driver's seat and tries to give travel directions.

The first problem is that our two young interpreters, neither of whom should have been on the trip in the first place, are not familiar with the route we are supposed to be taking. In fact, neither of them has ever been to the Tatras before.

Jan directs us off the main road to the small town of Nova Dubruka, which has a reputation for its Stalinist architecture. There is a pronounced, regimented feel about the place. Even the 'larger than life' sign at the entrance to the town smacks of Soviet imperialism. We are unsure whether Jan wants us to see this place as an example of good town planning, or as representing an era which Slovakia is leaving behind as it starts to embrace the capitalist system.

Shortly afterwards, we miss a turning off the highway to an outdoor village museum. Jan wants us to turn back. Martin, however, is of the view that we can visit this place on the way back. Lucy and Helena, as the linguistic go-betweens, feel they are in the firing line.

We approach the town of Zilina, which is down as a scheduled stop. No-one is giving clear directions to Chris the driver, who is losing his cool (unsurprisingly) for the first time on the entire tour. Eventually we find a coach park, from where we all make for the town centre on foot. By now, everyone is feeling stressed. Zilina is an industrial town, somewhat bigger than Trenčín, but it does not seem to have much beauty, at least in the parts that I see.

In the town centre we split up. Some of us, me included, have an interview arranged with a local architect at 11am. We have about half an hour to spare. Sarah and I decide to stride out and look for a bank to change money. I stop someone and ask the way to a bank, using my limited Slovak – I am *very* pleased with myself for making myself understood! I don't understand all of the reply, however, but we go in the direction the man points in and we think we catch the Slovak word for *"right turn"*. Eventually, we find a bank, but at that moment, Jan appears on the scene, takes us into an office, has a conversation with an official and then leads us out again. At this point, Sarah and I give him the slip, race round the block, and find another bank, where we do business.

While we are waiting for Tony to reappear and take us to our meeting with the local architects, we come across a half-dressed woman staggering around a newspaper kiosk and no-one appears to be trying to help her. She is clearly the worst for wear from the effects of alcohol. I ask Helena to try and get help. She goes to a nearby pharmacist and she is informed that the police know about her. Apparently, her daughter committed suicide by throwing herself off a 13th floor apartment balcony only two days before; all very distressing.

We walk for a couple of blocks further on and arrive for our scheduled meeting at the offices of a firm of local architects going by the name of Racional. We are taken around the offices by the principal architect, a Mr Sedlak, followed by a discussion with Helena interpreting. Jan also attends and there are times when he talks at the same time as the architect or Helena, and some of the answers to our questions consequently seem confusing.

Several points emerge from our meeting. We learn that the firm is a private company specialising in building design, interior design and the reconstruction/ refurbishment of buildings. They tell us that in the last five years they have specialised in banks, having designed 28 so far. Their turnover last year came to 60 million crowns (£1.2 million). They have also designed four churches which were built last year. (So, they are dealing with God as well as with mammon.) Up to 1990 they only got involved with new build schemes. Now, the emphasis is switching to renewal.

They tell us they are designing buildings all over Slovakia. However, there do not appear to be any development plans to provide a framework to guide where, when and how development might take place, or even what kinds of development and how much are needed – there appear to be some nationally based constraints on development, although these are not spelt out. There are stricter controls on development in historic centres and for some older buildings. The key determinant seems to be availability of infrastructure. There is also a form of building control in place. As in the UK, planning permissions are granted by local councils.

Until 1990 it was not possible under the Soviet administration to have private architectural practices in Slovakia. Mr Sedlak says he used to work in a state-run office; in 1990 he left the public sector and took 12 colleagues with him. There is much more freedom to design and develop now in the new world order in Slovakia; before 1990 every last detail was dictated from Bratislava. Now, most of the construction industry in Slovakia is privatised; capitalism has now got its feet under the table. Negotiating with individual companies rather than tendering is now the order of the day. However, only qualified people with certificates are permitted to design buildings for construction; it is not just left to anyone.

Despite Slovakia's new-found freedom, however, in recent years the country has been experiencing financial problems and many of Racional's smaller clients have felt the pinch. Someone in our group asks Mr Sedlak whether he is optimistic for the future here in Slovakia. Unlike the academics Tony saw in Bratislava University yesterday, Mr Sedlak says he is looking forward to an exciting and prosperous future for architecture in Slovakia. Time will tell who is right.

At the end of our question and answer session, everybody is given a ball pen, made in China. Tony and I are then singled out to receive calendars. My calendar displays pictures of buildings and townscapes. Tony, however, is presented with a girlie calendar, which he sheepishly accepts, to thunderous applause from the students. One of the students, Andy, manages to capture the moment on his camcorder. Once we are out in the street, Tony discards his calendar into the nearest rubbish bin. I think I shall keep mine.

We head out of Zilina at around half past one, following the Vah River Valley upstream. The valley becomes narrower and the scenery appears more attractive. Some of the mountains coming into view are snow-capped. The railway also follows the course of the river, running closely parallel to the road for long stretches. Jan continues to point out things of interest to me via Lucy.

Some of the towns in the Upper Vah Valley have a strong industrial character, and we pass by two armaments factories. Lucy explains that the Cold War arms market has been replaced by new demands from the Middle East. I think Slovakia is currently supplying arms to both Iraq and Iran in their high-casualty war against each other. Lucy says she is currently learning Arabic and produces a Slovak-Arabic grammar book from her bag, in case she thought I doubted her.

Shortly after a hydro-electric power project, we bypass a town with the name of Martin. Further on we see a paper mill. Jan says that the waste water from the mill is fed through pipes to heat the surrounding settlements (i.e. a combined heat and power scheme).

Further up the Vah Valley, the main road passes through a gorge. Two castles nestle precariously on limestone crags. After passing a cement works, we notice on the steep slopes a stretch of forest which appears to have been affected by acid rain; many of the trees are spindly, just wooden skeletons bereft of foliage. It seems to be quite localised, although Jan thinks it is caused by British or German industrial pollution. I tend to think that the nearby heavy industry in the Vah valley may have something to do with it.

Another electric train runs past us, and I remark on how impressed I am with what I have seen of the Slovak railway system. Lucy muses that I probably wouldn't say that if I actually had to travel in Slovak trains!

The road eventually breaks out of the valley and reaches a kind of steppe upland of fairly even terrain. There are distant views of the High Tatras Mountains to the north and the gentler, Low Tatras, some distance to the south. We are now travelling on a recently constructed stretch of motorway which as yet is not heavily used. Our late lunch stop is at a rest area which overlooks a lake – the Lipt Mara – which has a backdrop of snow-capped mountains. Martin says that later in the year, he plans to spend some of his summer holiday by the side of the lake.

We approach the ski resort town of Poprad in the early evening, after cancelling a visit to a wooden church, which again seems to result in tense discussions between Martin and our Slovak guides. Poprad, as the guide book says, is an *"unprepossessing"* town. Much of it comprises blocks of off-white 3-4 storey (and higher) flats, separated by featureless, barren open wedges, which deceptively look like attractive green areas on plans.

At our hotel, again there seems to be some tension, this time between Jan, the interpreters and the hotel owner. As usual, our two interpreters, Helena and Lucy, are caught in the middle and they seem to think that perhaps we are annoyed with them as well. They really are in an unfortunate situation.

Our group is divided between two hotels, which are in effect no more sophisticated than basic student hostels. Our two coach drivers take one look at their allocated accommodation – in our hostel! – and immediately decide to book into a 'proper' hotel.

Our group, which includes Tony and Helena, is driven to the opposite side of town from where Martin and his group will be staying, and we discover our 12-storey concrete monolith with primitive facilities. Morale among the students in our building reaches an all-time low, and Martin's name gets taken in vain by many of them. There is serious talk amongst some of the students of leaving for Trenčín first thing in the morning, although a preferred means of transport to get there is not mentioned. I seem to have drawn the short straw for deciding who goes in which room and I get to work drawing up a tabular list; fortunately, everyone seems happy with the particular arrangement we finish up with.

Later in the evening, we all meet up at a town centre restaurant and amazingly, our spirits revive over a good meal. Pavel, our waiter, is the son of the restaurant owners, and he makes a special effort to practise his English with us. When I ask him where I can find a telephone to make a call to England, he asks me to follow him through the kitchen, along a passage and then into his parents' living accommodation. He invites me to use his parents' phone and I manage to get through to my wife Sylvia first time on a very clear line, just before she goes off to play badminton. His parents then refuse to take any money for the phone call, at which point I wish I hadn't been talking to Sylvia on the phone for quite so long.

After the meal, the students discover one of the local night clubs. Sometime later, Pavel takes Tony and I around the town and eventually into the same nightclub, where we are bought several drinks by both the English and Slovak students. Returning hospitality in Slovakia seems to be very difficult. Pavel even takes us back to his place, where I make friends with his pet Alsatian dog, and then he drives us back to our hostel in his car, which is just as well because I have completely lost my bearings in this town.

Pavel is very keen to learn and improve his English. It is not surprising to me that so many young Slovaks want to learn the English language; it is their most obvious escape route to the West, which they perceive as a land of plenty, despite the fact that Communism no longer holds sway in the country.

Our ninth-floor hostel bedroom window looks out over a very well used railway. Freight (and a few passenger) trains continue to rumble along noisily until way into the small hours. At around one in the morning, some of our students return to the hotel/hostel in a state somewhere between happy and paralytic. Fortunately, their noise subsides fairly quickly, and our next challenge is going to be to wake them up at eight in the morning.

There has been no sign of Jan all evening. Initially, Jan, Tony and I are allocated one small bedroom between us. Tony and I, however, decide to occupy the adjacent room and we inform the hotel receptionist in the morning, who just accepts it without any questioning.

Saturday 8 April

WALKING IN THE HIGH TATRAS

The day starts badly when we discover, early in the morning, that one of our HNC students, Stuart, has cut his foot quite deeply on a broken bottle. Helena makes arrangements to get him into the local hospital and accompanies him, along with Tony.

The day gets worse when another HNC student, Andy, slips in the shower, although this turns out to be nothing more serious than bruising.

We also discover a pile of what I can only describe as an indescribable mess in the communal toilets in our hostel. All the external walls of our bedroom (and other bedrooms) are riddled with cracks, exposing clear views outside and letting in the cold temperature (around freezing). When I close one of the windows, the handle falls off. The students tell us that one of the hostel lifts broke down between the second and third floors during the night.

Our plan is to leave our hostel at eight in the morning in order to use the showers at Martin's more salubrious hostel, and then go on to have breakfast in our favourite town centre restaurant at 9:30 am. But Stuart's trip to hospital has delayed things somewhat and we do not finish breakfast until 11:00.

Eventually we set off for the High Tatras, which we have been able to locate from our hostel, albeit shrouded in mist. As we leave the tundra and enter a pine forest, it starts to snow. The coach parks up in the winter resort town of Stary Smokovec, in the Tatras National Park. Lucy has arranged for us to meet one of her friends from University, but a phone call reveals that all is not well for her at home, and she won't now be joining us.

We take the funicular railway up the side of a mountain after which we walk along the side of a forested valley towards a waterfall. It is snowing steadily, and our footpath is slippery and tortuous. A rather flimsy wooden barrier is all there is to prevent any major falls into a stream a long way below. Several of our party experience difficulties in making it on foot. Tony has several falls, one on his back, which he says is painful. Peggy, a student from Taiwan, exercises extreme caution in her movements, whilst Martin doesn't appear over-confident walking on snow and ice, and he moves along at a gingerly pace with a real look of angst. The views of the snow-capped peaks rising from the pine forest, however, are breathtaking. Several students are heard to comment that this walk in the mountains, which has an ethereal quality about it, has made the Slovakian tour worth it.

The climax of our walk is the waterfall itself. Water is pouring through a natural arch made in the snow, and I hope the photographs I am taking do it justice (they don't). With the gently falling snow, the sheer beauty of the mountain and forest landscape has a surreal quality. I am almost pinching myself to make sure this is not a figment of my imagination. I cannot recall a previous situation where I have seen and heard so many teenagers and young people go into ecstasies over a view.

Beyond the waterfall, in a forest clearing, snow fights, bumps, collisions, ambushes and general merriment become the order of the day. One snowball is hurled at me, accompanied by the student shouting: "*And that's for the bloody poll tax!*" Martin tells me that my being in the thick of the snowball fight is a sign of acceptance by the students; heaven help someone caught in the middle of a snow fight with these students who hasn't been accepted!

Back in the coach park, we learn that one group of students lost sight of the rest of the party, then took a ride on the narrow-gauge electric railway, thinking we had done so, before returning to the coach park. Apparently, they have been hanging around for ages, waiting for us to return. The rest of the students take great delight in explaining to this frustrated group what a fantastic walk to the waterfall they have just missed.

At around three in the afternoon, we are being driven along snow-covered roads to a frozen lake called Strbske Pleso, and we are encountering wind driven snow. After embarking from the coach, a 90-metre-high ski jump comes into view, but unfortunately there is no one in action. The sun comes out and the effects of the light on the trees, snow, rocks and ice is stunningly atmospheric and exhilarating, resulting in strong contrasts of light and shade. Again, I hope my photographs illustrate this (partly).

Peggy from Taiwan is finding it almost impossible to walk through the blinding snow once the wind gets up again, so she links arms with one of the students – Andy – and me, and we become a sort of phalanx. At one point, still linked together, Peggy walks backwards to minimise the impact of the snow.

We find refuge in a small café where I ask for white coffee in my best Slovak – and I am served with a black coffee! (Probably indicating my grasp of the Slovak language is not up to it.) Never mind, the coffee is hot and wet, and it tastes good, but there again, I am desperate for a drink. Most of us haven't eaten since breakfast, but even in the late afternoon, our hunger has been overtaken by exhilaration.

Back in the coach, we closely follow the track of a narrow-gauge electric railway, which connects Poprad and several other resorts in the Tatras, including the two places we visit today. Our coach is forced to stop at a level crossing to allow a train to pass, with the train sounding its klaxon to signify its right of way. Ray, our driver, and never one to miss an opportunity, responds to the train with his horn. This is followed by much waving between the passengers on the coach and the train, and the train driver cannot conceal a broad grin. Once the train has passed through the level crossing, Ray then races to get to the next level crossing before the train, and as he overtakes the train, he shouts: "*Get a new engine!*" Several funicular railways and chairlifts are served by this electric railway.

On one of the snowfields that we visit at our next stop, an over-familiar German from the former GDR (East Germany) insists on telling me, in German, how everything now is so much more expensive in capitalist Slovakia since the end of Communism. Fortunately, Lucy's German is up to interpreting what he says, or I would have been sunk completely. Lucy and I also think that the German guy is a little intoxicated (and not just on Communism).

Jan, our guide, is still at loggerheads with Lucy and Helena, especially as we have changed our plans this morning. Sarah, Tony and I have been trying to keep out of Jan's way, partly because he always makes a beeline for us, but also because he has several unfortunate habits or traits, such as talking at you, which often includes interrupting you when we are in the middle of a conversation with someone else. He also chain smokes. Yesterday at dinner, I had smoke blown continually in my face from Jan's cigarette.

On the funicular railway which we rode on earlier today, I confess to hiding from him half way down the train, where I am surrounded by students, so that I am all but invisible. Jan, however, then gets Lucy to find me; our students think this is hilarious.

Talking of the students, I have encountered nothing but friendliness from them, none of whom I knew before embarking on this trip. Several of them have come up to me and introduced themselves, and a lot of them approach me and chat casually. Peggy has written a question that she wants me to put to the local Council in Trenčín when we meet up with the civic leaders next Monday. The question covers planning policies for high-rise flats. Come to think of it, why doesn't she want to ask the question herself?

In the late afternoon, we travel back to Poprad. Although utilitarian blocks of flats are widespread throughout the town, we pass through an area of new semi-detached and terraced two-storey housing with good brickwork and pleasant pitched roofs, near to the airport, to the north of the railway station; signs of the new post-Soviet Slovakia catering to the burgeoning demands of a growing middle class.

Poprad also displays a lot of neglect and dilapidation, and an obvious sign is the condition of many of the street kerbs and pavements that are generally uneven and sometimes broken (not a good place to push a wheelchair). If the hostel where we are staying in is anything to go by, much of the high-rise development is crying out for major repair works and renovation, and some of the students are of the opinion that our hostel building would be classified as a dangerous structure back in the UK.

At our evening meal, Tony draws the short straw and sits next to 'Ivan the Terrible', as we are now nick-naming him. Sarah is having great difficulty in keeping a straight face over this. After dinner, the students want to try Poprad's other night clubs, and they invite us to accompany them. We discover at the door that strangers have to pay double the Slovakian price to gain admission, but it is still less than one pound sterling. Peggy argues the toss but loses. The students only stay for about half an hour and then decide to head for a bar.

I also come away from the nightclub early and I walk alone through the nearly deserted streets. There are virtually no cars on the roads, except for a couple of roving police cars, whilst the railway seems to be busier than the road (and noisier).

Back in the hostel, Tony is getting more concerned about his wife's pregnancy and the fact that he has been unable to make telephone contact with her. It is now 12:40 am and three passenger trains have just clattered into Poprad station, all from the east.

The students are quieter tonight than on previous nights. Some have run out of money and several are tired. Stuart, the student who put his foot through the broken glass, needed five stitches, but the bandaging seems good. He and Andy are recovering well. Helena feels ill today (or was it yesterday?) and she has spent the entire day in Poprad; you have to be ill to want to spend the entire day in Poprad.

This day has also included a few linguistic surprises for me. One of the older students, Steve, has apparently managed to get a grasp of Slovak grammar, thanks to an embassy friend. Andy tells me he has taken lessons in Thai and is now studying Japanese. Another student, Paul, tells me over dinner that he is fluent in German and demonstrates this by ordering a pint of pivo for me in German. Ray, one of our coach drivers, says he can speak Polish, but do I believe him?

Sunday 9 April

THE LOW TATRAS AND THE 'FOSSILISED' VILLAGE OF CICIMANI

Everyone is feeling tired – one snow fight and several pivos too many, I suspect. Looking out over the town of Poprad from the vantage point of our hostel bedroom, we see that it has been snowing and everywhere has a light, white covering.

On the way to our breakfast rendezvous in the town centre, we see many people in the streets who are dressed formally; this is the Sunday commute to church.

After breakfast, our coach pulls out of Poprad and we head for the caves at Správa Slovenskych Jaskyn, to the south of Denanova in the Nizks (Lower) Tatry Mountains. The coach follows in the wake of a snowplough for much of the way. Then, when the road looks clearer, we come up behind a car which starts to indicate left, moves into the centre of the road and then, just as our coach commits to passing on the right, goes into a skid and moves across the road towards our coach. The quick response of Chris, our driver, showing good presence of mind, saves the day – he accelerates and just misses the car, which eventually ends up on our side of the road again, but mercifully behind us.

We arrive at one of the cave entrances in deep snow; and it's another excuse for a snowball fight. Our walk through the cave system is two kilometres long and we scale just under one thousand steps and cross several subterranean bridges. The cave is impressive and full of contrasts in the way the limestone has weathered.

At the deepest point in the cave we encounter a swift flowing stream, which seems to me to be comparable in volume to the River Dart above Postbridge on Dartmoor. We come across several isolated pools, one apparently six metres deep. The lighting effects are well done; not too garish. At one point, the track leads through a forest of limestone columns; our route is convoluted, and the joined-up stalagmites and stalactites are so densely packed that we are forced to walk single file. There is even an area of dying stalagmites, where a rock fall which occurred a few thousand years ago has cut off their supply of calciferous water.

The caves, apparently, were discovered by two boys in the 1820s, and they carried out their exploration by candlelight. In the late nineteenth century, one of Europe's most famous composers, Smetner, spent some time in the cave seeking inspiration.

We exit the cave and adjust our eyes to the bright open sky. Almost immediately the snowball fights resume. The Slovak students can't understand why the snow is so exciting for our students. Martin comes in for some victimisation as he is pelted by snowballs from all directions, and then it's my turn; no mercy is shown to either of us.

As we drive back along the narrow valley and then onto the main highway, there is some debate over whether or not to use chains for the coach. There is virtually no traffic on the main highway, in total contrast to the crowded German autobahns of last Sunday. We carry on without using chains.

We head for Cicimani, which is a traditional and well preserved Slovakian village. It is a national treasure. On the left of the coach there is a spectacular snow-covered mountain. Martin sees if any of the students are gullible by announcing that we are passing the Matterhorn on our left! One of the students, Jason, then remarks:" *Did you know that 'Ski Sunday' is coming from here next week?"*

As well as being well preserved, Cicimani is an 'open air' museum. Much of the village comprises wooden houses, some rebuilt since the last great fire in 1921 (Martin remembers aloud that 1921 was the year – the only year – that his football team, West Bromwich Albion – won the English football league [Not many people in Slovakia know this...]).

All the houses have ornate hand carvings on the outer walls and a few of us enter one of these houses, which has been preserved as a museum piece. Inside, there are traditional costumes and domestic implements, with records going back to 1271. The ability to secure leather, wool and wood from within the community ensured a sustainable way of life for centuries, with almost no need for the villagers to trade. It is a pleasant contrast to see pictures of ladies in white costumes, as opposed to the black apparel of many Catholic communities in southern Europe.

An elderly couple invite Martin, Steve and I into their home and we buy some traditional embroidery from them. Walking back to our coach, which admittedly could do with a wash, I notice that a number of inscriptions have been fingered on the back, including:

"*Pivo tour 95*"
"*Also available in white*"
"*Bolton Wanderers 1, WBA 0*"

There are also one or two descriptions of what I suspect is rather dubious Slovak, and I dread to think what the translations are.

Driving back to Trenčín is like a homecoming. We are almost ecstatic at leaving Poprad. Sarah, whose diction, manners and sense of propriety are immaculate, describes Poprad as: "*unprepossessing – in other words a shithole*". Feelings have run high over several aspects of our stay there, and without a doubt the 'fairyland' snow and the impressive mountain scenery have saved the weekend. The first glimpse of Trenčín Castle, silhouetted against the late afternoon sky, is a wonderful sight.

In the evening, Martin and I invite Lucy out for a meal, to thank her for all her hard work as an interpreter. She wants us to go to Mike's Bar (she thinks it's appropriate for some reason). However, when we order drinks, we discover that the place has no beer; Martin pulls Lucy's leg mercilessly over this.

Before too long, we progress to the decidedly up-market Hotel Tatra, where apparently, South Devon College is organising a conference this autumn. Martin tackles Lucy over the Slovakian attitude towards gypsies, and Lucy is careful in her reply, but the general gist is that gypsies are not entirely welcome in Slovakia. Drinks are served, and we don't allow Lucy to pay for anything, which isn't easy; Slovak generosity is legendary. Before leaving the hotel, we ascend to the first floor and peer through a window onto the Latin plaque set in a rock face. It commemorates the famous Roman victory of Marcus Aurelius in AD 179.

At a third bar we meet up with Sarah and Tony. I restrict myself to coffees. Then we move on to a bar near the station. Lucy by this time is refusing to drink anything more, so Sarah buys her a pint of Pivo. Lucy only agrees to drink it if we agree to drink some of it as well. I am beginning to think Lucy is being pressured (in the nicest possible way), so when it is my turn, I drink most of the glass. Lucy then pours heaps of sugar into the remnant of the beer in the glass and downs it.

The conversation somehow moves onto star signs. I initially keep quiet on this subject, but eventually I am asked for my views. I kill conversation by stating my total aversion to astrology and refusing to let the others know the date of my birthday. At around midnight we manage to persuade Lucy to take a taxi and the rest of us walk back to our hostel. Lucy agrees to meet me at ten o'clock tomorrow morning to help me with my shopping for presents.

I have a sleepless night. I close my bedroom window and it is too hot. I then open it sometime later and nearly freeze to death. It is now snowing in Trenčín.

Monday 10 April

QUESTIONS AT THE TOWN HALL AND A FASHION SHOW

In the morning of our last full day in Slovakia, most of the students go off to look at a construction site in Trenčín. Instead of doing this, I walk into the town centre and wander around the shops on my own. Lucy has agreed to meet me at ten, to interpret for me in the shops. I have ideas for my sons, Nathan and David, but I'm less clear about what to buy for my wife, Sylvia. I walk into the main square at ten and Lucy is already there.

I apologise to Lucy for feeling like a zombie, as I am very tired (partly from a semi-sleepless night). Lucy seems wide awake, though. We set off shopping. The first few shops we visit don't even sell men's clothes; I am after sweat shirts for the boys. Is this shopping trip going to be disastrous?

We eventually find something in one shop – the shopkeeper says she worked in Spain and we managed to communicate a little. In most of the shops, Lucy is very dismissive of the quality of goods on offer, and although she is obviously speaking to me in English, it must be obvious to the Slovak sales assistants that she is not over impressed!

I suggest we go for a coffee and we end up in Mike's Bar again – the 'dry', pivo-less bar of the night before. We talk about some of the foster children who live in Children's Town where Lucy lives, and I agree to try and find English pen friends for three sisters (Andrea, Petra and Kate) whose father is in prison. We talk quite a lot about English expressions and she asks me to write a few of them down on paper. She tells me that her English is not very good – and she thinks I am winding her up when I try to assure her that it is really good. She dismisses me as a *"funny Englishman"*.

She also queries me about my reluctance the previous evening to want to reveal my star sign and we talk briefly about my Christian beliefs. She says that her Catholic beliefs are very different from mine, and for some reason I decide to let this go.

After another bout of shopping, Lucy suggests that we go for a pizza. She tells me that she hasn't been to this restaurant before and she wants to know what my view is of the place. The pizza, as it turns out, is not the best that I have ever tasted – it is obvious to me that no Italian has had a hand in making it. Lucy asks whether I like it or not, and I am sure she would have walked out if I had been too critical. I say that it is "interesting"; she smiles. We then talk about holidays. She says that her parents said that I would be welcome to stay at their place if ever I come back to Slovakia on holiday. She says she is keen for me to visit Prague, and also enquires as to the cost of English courses at South Devon College, although she seems doubtful whether she could ever be able to afford to come over and study English in the UK.

The pre-arranged time to meet at the local authority Planning Department is 12:30. We leave the pizzeria at 12:25, and I notice Martin standing outside the Town Hall looking worried. As soon as he sees me, he gesticulates for me to come with him immediately. Apparently, the meeting with the Chief Planning Officer has already begun. I feel somewhat frustrated, dash into the Town Hall, and make my entrance into the meeting, which is in full swing, with Beata interpreting.

All is not lost, however, and I manage to put several questions to the Chief Planner, including Peggy's on high-rise flats. The main points which arise during the meeting are amplified for me by information whispered to me by Tony on what has been discussed before I arrived.

Firstly, we are informed that the Council is drawing up new plans for Trenčín, which will take three years to prepare. The new Plan aims to make provision for a population increase based on a forecast of around an additional 35,000 people over a period of 15 years or so; this is around half the rate of growth envisioned in the previous plan, and the slowdown in growth is based on a lower rate of industrialisation than was previously thought. So, the new development plan is already moving away from the over-ambitious population and economic targets set in Soviet times.

The Plan also takes Trenčín's tourism potential seriously; a detailed conservation study is being drawn up covering around 200 buildings in the town centre; however, some of the land in this area is in disputed ownership, which is hampering progress.

In terms of new growth for the town, there are also four slightly ominously entitled 'zones of control', which are in effect designated new housing areas.

The Draft new Development Plan for Trenčín will go on deposit for a month, to tap into the public mood, and if there is a response from the people, and even better, support for the plan, then it will be approved, so we are told. Interestingly, the planners indicate an approval rating of 55% as the threshold above which they will approve the plan. It is unclear to me whether an Inquiry will take place, but I rather think not.

Trenčín's planners tell us that the implementation of development plans in Slovakia is beset by financial problems, and they tell us that they think implementation issues are easier for us in the West! (Little do they know…)

The effects of major out-of-town shopping developments are beginning to be recognised in Slovakia, and I am not surprised that a study on the effects of an out-of-town store on the town of Zilina, not far to the north of Trenčín, is currently being undertaken.

I find it interesting that the local council in Trenčín sets its targets for new housing completions independently of central government. There would appear to be no centralised guidance or housing targets set by Bratislava.

We are informed that the development of new public sector housing can only be financed by sales of state-owned properties and land. At this point I can't help but inform them that in Britain we can only spend up to a maximum of half the capital receipts for this purpose, as the remainder has to go on repaying debt charges.

Conversation turns to high-rise housing. We are informed that multi-storey flats were introduced in Slovakia in the 1950s and really caught on the 1960s. In those days, the Communist authorities dictated housing densities, top down, very strictly, with no freedom to introduce any variations. After 1990, the entire issue of multi-storey housing was re-examined and whilst the development of high-rise flats continues, it is stressed that now there is more variation in heights, styles and house types. The number of storeys is generally being reduced in new developments, from an average of 8-10 storeys to around 4-5. This is said to be a significant relaxation from the previous hard-line policy on tall buildings.

It is clear from the comments made that the Council here in Trenčín recognises the importance of planning for communities, as opposed to building just housing estates, which seems to have been the ethos of the previous Soviet era. Plans aim to improve the quality of life through the provision of social, recreational and sporting facilities, subject of course to the availability of finances.

Another interesting development is the use of architectural competitions; something which they tell us is being pursued actively.

The substantial tract of wooded hillside adjacent to the castle is being protected from development in the public interest. There was a plan to develop the town around the woodland, but this has now been abandoned, and appropriately so in my judgment.

At the end of the formal question and answer session I am introduced to the chief planner of Trenčín (perhaps the Borough Architect or Engineer might be a more accurate job title). I present him with a copy of the Torbay Local Plan, and spend a short time highlighting some of the main themes and issues in the plan. The Slovak officials are fascinated with the shape of Torbay's coastline, something I tend to take for granted, but coming from residents of a land-locked nation, perhaps I shouldn't have been that surprised.

Time does not allow for a full in-depth dialogue on the many planning issues that we have in common. I am requested to write my name and address inside the cover of the plan. Perhaps the dialogue will continue?

The editor of the local newspaper, whom I bumped into almost a week ago last Tuesday, then asks me if I would write an article on my first impressions of Trenčín. I agree to do this, and he gives me his business card. For the first name I now know his name; Ivan Slavík.

Our meeting with the Trenčín planners is over all too quickly, and there is hardly time to peruse a large-scale map of the local municipal area which has been displayed for our benefit. It looks like a typical policies map which would form part of a development plan back in the UK.

Later in the day, Martin expresses an interest in submitting an article on the links between our two colleges, to go in the local newspapers. Lucy also asks me if she could have a copy of my article. My writing has never been in such demand!

We leave the Town Hall and I spend the afternoon walking around the town centre, buying the remainder of my presents to take home with me. It is now gloriously hot, despite last night's snow. In my town centre perambulations, I bump into several of our students. Some are on the trail of Jason, who has 'disappeared' owing (allegedly) significant amounts of money; others talk of being offered 'joints' in a night club the previous evening – and then they point out the pusher, who is shuffling, in a low-profile sort of way, through the town square.

Later I meet up with Tony, also looking for presents, and we have a coffee together in Mike's Bar (where else?) and then visit the bank to change money. The bank refuses to accept one of my £20 notes, on the grounds that it has a very small tear. Fortunately, I have a 'perfect' one to enable me to complete the transaction. I then complete my present purchases, buying Sylvia some perfume (which is probably a high-risk strategy). The lady sales assistant makes up a beautifully wrapped work of art out of the coloured wrapping paper. She then asks me how to say some Slovak expressions in English. Shopping is almost fun in Slovakia!

I make my way slowly back to our hostel under the weight of my presents, meeting on the way two further students, Ashley and James, who tell me they have enjoyed the trip. Ashley says that he only has to speak English in the centre of Trenčín, and girls start coming up to speak to him (this experience never happens to me!).

After completing my final packing back in the hostel, I then leg it over the road to where the evening's farewell celebrations are going to be held.

There is a change of plan, however. Instead of leaving for home first thing in the morning, the idea now is to depart from Trenčín immediately after tonight's final get-together with all the students, including a disco, so I am informed. Martin says the aim is to leave by ten o'clock, which strikes me as verging on the optimistic.

The celebrations kick off soon after five in the evening, and they go on for a long time. Tickets are on sale for the students' fashion show, but being long in the toothski, they let me in for free.

The first part of the evening is relatively formal. We are assigned places at tables. Martin and Beata are seated in prime positions on the top table. Lucy is invited up onto the top table to help in interpretation and sits between Martin and me. Sarah and Tony sit immediately to my left.

We have a great view of an excellent fashion show (not that I possess any relevant qualifications to make a sound judgment on this subject, but it is colourful and lively, and the music is easy to listen to). Martin and Beata make presentations to the students afterwards. Lucy is concerned about Helena, who has disappeared for a time and now appears very down. After discussing each of the models as they strut along the catwalk, Lucy asks me if my wife is fair haired – an interesting and perceptive observation.

After the presentations and the food, the disco starts up and it is, unsurprisingly, noisy. This is the obvious cue for the senior figures (at least in age) to retreat into a small room, where various lethal drinks are lined up for us; I succeed, however, in avoiding the 40% borrovitchka. Mr Strubner, the college principal, joins us, together with several teachers, as well as some of the students who are avoiding the disco.

Far from being a boring alternative to the disco, there is a lot of animated discussion in the side room. I am introduced to Katarina, an undergraduate architecture student from the University of Bratislava, and the daughter of Victor, one of the senior lecturers of the college here in Trenčín. She is initially quiet, but soon starts to talk about her course, her impressions of the city of Bratislava, and her views on the future of architecture, on which subject she is quite optimistic.

I am also introduced to the college secretary and to one of the German teachers. I touch upon the controversial topic of whether the Czech Republic and Slovakia should be reunited. Our small group is split down the middle on this issue, with some expressing the view that Slovakia is too small to be a sustainable national unit, with others arguing that the top jobs and prestige development would nearly always go to the Czechs in a united country, which can't be right for Slovakia. Lucy interprets virtually simultaneously – she is so good at it that she even inserts a sentence or two of her own at the end, such as: "*Well, that's her opinion, but I don't agree with it*".

A bright 16 years old student, by the name of Kate, who attends a neighbouring school (the Gymnasium) and who is the daughter of the German teacher, also has a go at interpreting at one point. She is against the idea of the two countries merging and, like her mother, is staunchly pro-nationalist. I think that if ever Lucy becomes a politician, she will fight for reunification.

We eventually succumb to pressure from the students and drag ourselves out of the side room and onto the disco dance floor; the disco is now in full swing. Martin gets boxed in by the students, forming a circle around him. He doesn't appear to be protesting too much, me thinks. I think Nadine, one of the Slovak students, is the main culprit. Apparently, so I am told, the music is "*technics*" in its genre. (This does not mean a lot to me.) Lucy says she doesn't like it – she seems to have quite definite views on most things!

The time draws near for us to leave Trenčín and Slovakia. Lucy insists on walking home (perhaps two miles away) and no one can persuade her to take a taxi. Even Beata thinks I am fussing over nothing of any significance. The only thing Lucy will accept is my loose Slovak change, which amounts to about one-pound sterling, and even then, she asks why I don't change it in a bank!

A lot of goodbyes are said. Crowds are there to see us off. One of the students, Ian, takes ten minutes longer to 'say' goodbye to his young lady friend than anyone else, and nearly gets left behind as the coach starts to move away from the college.

Eventually, the coach leaves the college at a quarter to midnight, with Chris at the wheel, to the sound of the Jam singing "*I'm in love, I'm in love!*" I think I've fallen in love with Slovakia.

Tuesday 11 April

A SPOT OF BOTHER IN NÜRNBERG

We drive through the Austrian border control in the small hours. Ray then takes over and drives through the night, and we arrive in Nürnberg at ten in the morning. A sense of anti-climax and tiredness sets in. We are informed that we can't enter the youth hostel until midday, so we force ourselves to walk around the cite centre and find out last week's English football results.

We manage to catch up on some rest on our bunk beds in the afternoon, not before time. Martin gives away tell-tale signs that he is sleeping for at least some of the time. After our evening meal, Martin and I stroll around the castle walls, and later we join Sarah and Tony in a nearby bar.

My aim is to go to bed early and catch up on a good night's sleep. It doesn't quite work out like that. Firstly, our students return to the youth hostel, some quite noisily and a number definitely the worst for wear. Jason in particular is highly excited about a sex show act that he has just seen, where he feels he has been short changed. His quote goes along the lines of: "*This woman, when she stripped, had a 'what's it', honest!*" There are times when I think Jason is 23 going on 12.

Later, in the small hours, it's the German's turn to shatter the peace. A tinny sounding radio, coming from way beneath us in the bowels of the castle, is loud enough to disturb the sleep of the entire place. By three o'clock, I can't stand it any longer. To the amusement of the others in our dormitory, I hasten down to the source of the cacophony, several floors below.

On reaching the room where the sound is coming from – and it isn't difficult to discern which room it is - I hammer on the door, which I discover is unlocked as it crashes open. In a surreal couple of minutes, I get a view of a dark room as I shout at a bewildered skinny German youth, who leaps out of his bed in his boxer shorts and stands to attention, almost saluting me. There are muffled female groans coming from the bed in the background. In my best German, I shout "*Schlafen, schnell!*" (Sleep, quickly!) and then slam the door shut. The radio falls silent.

I return to my bedroom in what is now a quiet youth hostel. Tony and Martin tell me later that they were killing themselves laughing, as I could be clearly heard all over the hostel.

Wednesday 12 April

CROSSING WESTERN EUROPE

An early start would have been even earlier if Ashley hadn't remembered, in the thick of the Nürnberg rush hour that he had left his camera back at the youth hostel. Ray, our driver, is not a happy bunny at this point.

An uneventful journey across Germany, which is pleasant enough but we are tired, is punctuated by a superb view of Cologne Cathedral with its twin spires, as the coach crosses the River Rhine.

Belgium looks almost interesting in the setting sun. We drive on into France and through the outer suburbs of Lille. We arrive at Calais in time to do some shopping in a retail warehouse.

Our night crossing of the English Channel is calm, and we enjoy a hot meal on the ferry at something past midnight. Martin, Tony, Sarah and I recall some of the more amusing comments made during the past ten days. I include some of these in my postscript.

Thursday 13 April

RETURN TO ALBION

We are in serious danger of arriving in Torquay too early. As we wait to disembark at Dover, Ray winds up all the other motorists by sounding his horn, and they all follow like sheep. He really is a manipulator!

At seven o'clock in the morning, Torquay is still bathing in bright sunshine when the coach draws up outside the college and everyone disembarks. A final group photograph is taken, and then off I trot, perhaps not bright-eyed and bushy-tailed, ready to face another exciting day in the Torbay Planning Department.

Postscript

COMMENTS MADE BY STUDENTS AND STAFF ON THE PIVO TOUR

"*Are we in Germany yet?*" – Sarah waking up after a deep slumber on the outward journey, just as the coach was about to cross into Austria.

"*Is this buffalo urine?*" – Tony's reaction to his first experience of Slovakian tea.

"*After three bus journeys and then a two-mile hike, my arms were dropping off. This has got to be a wind up!*" - One of the students (Shane) describing his eventful journey to his host family, who apparently lived 'some distance from college', on the first evening.

"*Well, the sign said Bratislava*" – Martin's comments regarding the directions given to the coach drivers as we approached the Slovak border. Unfortunately, the party was then heading for Budapest!

"*Let's get pivoed-up!*" – Sarah showing she had mastered the Slovak language by the first evening!

"*Peggy, that hat doubles your heigh*t" – The Torbay Planning Officer's truthful observation!

"*My leg just gave way*"- One of the students' (Andy) excuse for falling off the pool table in mid shot in Trenćín.

"*Ow, my chest!*" – Hardman Jason's reaction to being 'clothes-lined' by Sarah in the football competition.

"*Where the hell did this banana come from!*" – Chris waking up one morning to find bananas stuffed in every pocket by his 'mates'.

"*That's the only thing you'll pull all week, Ray!*" – Sympathetic remark from Chris to his co-driver when Ray pulled his hamstring playing in the football competition.

"*I was doing the crawl and it just popped out*" – Leigh's explanation of how to dislocate your shoulder whilst swimming!

"*What broken glass?*" – Words spoken a split second before Stuart trod on broken glass and received five stitches in Poprad hospital.

"*That last train has 39 bogeys*" – Mike and Tony listening to the nightlife outside their bedroom in Poprad.

"*That's for the bloody poll tax!*" – Comment that accompanied a snowball with some venom at Mike.

"*We're on the 11th floor and there's a foot gap all the way round the room!*" – Another complaint about the accommodation in Poprad.

"*This place sucks!*" – Philosophical observation on Poprad.

"*I'm going to get you, Miss!*" – Words Ashley wished he had never uttered to Sarah in the midst of the snowball war.

"*Once you speak English, all the girls look at you*" – Ashley suddenly finding himself attractive to the opposite sex.

"*Is this for endurance?*" – Adam on receiving his certificate from the Head of Trenčín College.

"*If you look through the back window, you'll get the best view of Trenčín*" – Our driver-cum-comedian Ray's comment as we left Trenčín on the last day.

"*I thought the mountains were the highlight until tonight*" – Hardman Jason's comment after watching the superb fashion show on our last evening.

"*You never see a fat Slovak girl, do you?*" – No, you don't.

"*Where's the tent, Pegs?*" – Martin's comments directed at Peggy's walking wigwam!

www.ingramcontent.com/pod-product-compliance
Lightning Source LLC
Chambersburg PA
CBHW060343080526
44584CB00013B/902